Gay and (

Yes!

Rev. William H. Carey

Third Edition

© 2006, 2008, 2017 Lighthouse Ministries

978-1-387-17898-8

Dedication

This work is dedicated first and foremost to our Lord and Savior, Jesus Christ, the only wise God. It is further dedicated to the many LGBTQ people seeking truth amid the confusion and condemnation so prevalent in Christianity today. My prayer is that you may be reconciled to God, knowing that He created you, and loves you, *as you are.*

Table of Contents

Ch.		Pg.
1	Errors in the Bible?.....................................	1
2	Adam & Eve vs. Adam & Steve...................	21
3	The Sin of Sodom Wasn't What You Think.....	29
4	Leviticus 18:22..	45
5	Leviticus 20:13..	53
6	Romans...	61
7	1 Corinthians & 1 Timothy.........................	67
8	Same-Sex Marriage in Scripture..................	77
9	Transgender..	95

Errors in the Bible?

In the original autographs, written between c. 1312 BC[1] and c. AD 96[2], the actual original copies written down by the prophets and apostles, we believe there were no errors that could affect doctrine. But from that point on, human error was bound to creep in. Still, in looking at the Hebrew text of the Old Testament, we can easily see how very careful the Jewish people have been over the millennia to preserve the text. One way we see this is that original errors have not been corrected. When we say 'original errors,' we are not talking about potential doctrinal errors. We're talking about simple errors of spelling and grammar.

Those to whom God originally gave His word did not have dictionaries or thesauruses handy to verify spellings or meanings. It's not at all uncommon to find more than one spelling of Hebrew words in the Old Testament, as well as misspellings. The writings of Moses are a good example. Moses was a Hebrew, but had not been raised in a Jewish household. From his infancy, he had been raised as the son of

---

[1] Spiro, Rabbi Ken. Crash Course in Jewish History. Targum Press 2010. Chapter 9.

[2] Mounce, Robert. The Book of Revelation (revised ed.). The New International Commentary on the New Testament Series. Cambridge, UK: Eerdmans. pp. 15-16.

Pharaoh's daughter. He knew he was a Jew by birth, but had not been brought up in the knowledge of his people or their language. Undoubtedly, he had received the finest education Egypt could provide, being a member of the royal family. So he would have been fluent in Egyptian, and have known their arts and sciences, but not so with his own history and language.

Moses mentions being slow of speech and slow of tongue. He was particularly concerned about going to his own people and telling them that God had sent him. Many have taken this to mean that Moses had some kind of speech impediment. While this cannot be ruled out, more than likely what he meant was that he simply didn't know Hebrew well enough to be a good spokesman for God to the Jewish people. And in reading his written Hebrew, we do occasionally find errors of grammar. They don't affect his meaning in the slightest; they're just grammatically incorrect.

God does not generally dictate His word verbatim. If He did, the entire Bible would be in one writing style. But it is not. Rather, He gave the message, in detail, and allowed each writer to phrase it in his own words and style. But the most significant thing about the various errors of spelling and grammar in the Hebrew Old Testament isn't the fact that they occurred, but the fact that they have never been corrected.

The Jewish people have such reverence for the word of God that they will not make even the slightest alteration to the text, not even to correct a simple and obvious error. Instead, they have means of pointing out the errors, without correcting them. A Jewish sofer (scribe) has a very difficult and demanding job. It is this man's responsibility to copy over the scrolls of the Tanakh (Old Testament) by hand. Every single letter must be written absolutely perfectly. If there is even the slightest error, whether a misshapen letter, an error in spelling by the sofer, or even a stray dot of ink on the page, the entire page is invalid and may not be used. Corrections, erasures, etc., are not permitted. With that kind of attention and reverence, it's quite easy to believe that the Hebrew Old Testament says today pretty much exactly what it said 2400 years ago when the last book was penned.

While those preserving the Greek New Testament have never shown that much attention to detail, we still have a pretty good situation: although there are different manuscripts, and there are some small differences, they aren't significant enough for the most part to cause doctrinal error. (This is speaking only of the oldest manuscripts. In the 16th century, an altered Greek manuscript appeared on the scene, created not by copying over older Greek manuscripts, but by translating part of a flawed Latin translation back into Greek.

This manuscript was known as the *Textus Receptus* ["received text"]. For some reason, the translators of the King James Version chose to reject EVERY ancient Greek New Testament available to them, and to use only newer manuscripts, relying heavily on the flawed *Textus Receptus*. This has indeed led to some error, including a fraudulent verse found in several English [and other vernacular] translations. This will be explained later in this chapter.)

While God has indeed preserved His word to a remarkable degree in the original languages, enabling us the potential for an accurate translation, that is, sadly, as far as His protection has gone. It cannot be said to extend to the various vernacular translations, because it is easy to see that those various versions frequently disagree with each other, often significantly. Why are there errors? Why did (and do) translators take liberties?

The answers to these questions vary from century to century. The earliest known deliberate tampering with the word is traced back to late versions of the Latin Vulgate in the 9th century.[3] In those days, it was monks in monasteries who were charged with copying over translations of Christian Bibles. The only permitted language at the time was Latin. And for centuries, the Vulgate had been copied over by hand,

---
[3] Newcome, William. "The New Testament in an Improved Version." (Boston reprinting of the London ed.) Boston: Thomas B. Wait. 1809.

prior to the invention of the printing press. But even after the press was invented, the practice of hand lettering manuscripts continued. And for the most part, this practice produced no significant problems... until the day some anonymous monk decided to add his own words to one of the manuscripts. We don't know who he was, what his motives were, or exactly when he did it. What we do know is this: all of a sudden, there was a 9th century manuscript of John's first epistle with an extra verse in it. This verse, known today as the Johannine Comma, breaks the sense of the passage, as it does not follow the line of thought John was expressing. But there it was. And in later years, when that manuscript was copied over to produce a new one, that verse was innocently copied right along with it. (More on that later in this chapter.)

There wasn't the kind of biblical scholarship then that we would find today. Were a new Bible to appear today with an added verse, it wouldn't take long at all for people to notice. But back when this new verse was first added, the chances that anyone would notice were remarkably small. Only clergy were allowed to have copies of the Bible, and those copies were only in Latin, which only the educated few could read. People were not allowed to study scripture for themselves. And since there weren't multiple copies to choose from, the chances that any one priest would have two manuscripts to compare weren't good. Now, had this error been confined only to the Latin Vulgate, it might not have been a problem for later translations. But it didn't work out that way.

In 1516, Desiderius Erasmus published a printed version of the Greek New Testament. Although largely based on the much older Byzantine manuscripts, there was one very significant difference: Erasmus compared the Byzantine to the late flawed versions of the Vulgate, and he incorporated the errors of the Vulgate into his new Greek manuscript. This new, now flawed, Greek manuscript came to be known as the *Textus Receptus*.

It is not uncommon to hear proponents of the King James Version (also known as the Authorized Version) use the *Textus Receptus* as the basis for their claim that only that version is accurate and should be used. Those making this claim are generally unaware that the Textus Receptus is only a New Testament manuscript, and are also usually unaware that it was only about 100 years old when the KJV was translated, or that it was altered to agree with late versions of the Latin Vulgate. They are also unaware that the KJV translators chose to reject the numerous more ancient and authoritative Greek manuscripts of the New Testament that were available, and based their work largely on the Textus Receptus and other relatively recent manuscripts. That was not divine guidance or a wise decision. It resulted in KJV containing the added verse of the anonymous scribe copying over the Vulgate.

1 John 5:7, as found in the King James Version and several other versions, is a known fraud. This verse cannot be found in ANY ancient Greek manuscript, nor in any of the early Latin translations. It was never cited in any way by the Church Fathers, even at times when doing so would have been of great advantage to them. Clearly, the Church Fathers never heard of it. It breaks the sense of what John was writing about, and is without scriptural authority. The King James Version translators, if they didn't actually know that, SHOULD have known it: Had they consulted any ancient Greek manuscripts, they would have known the verse was absent from all of them. Either they didn't consult those manuscripts, or chose to ignore them.

Some new versions leave the verse out altogether, while others include it only in a footnote. But what is truly baffling is that the new versions of KJV [NKJV, KJV21] continue to include this verse, despite the facts concerning it, and the fact that no legitimate Bible scholar in the world believes John wrote it.

Another factor involved in errors in vernacular translations of the Bible applies to the earlier versions. The earliest translations were sponsored by churches (Lutheran into German, Anglican into English, Catholic into English and French, etc.) One thing all these churches taught, despite their dislike for each other and doctrinal differences, is that the church was to be the final arbiter of doctrine, not the Bible. Today, not many Christian people would agree with that, yet it is still in practice, and even in actual doctrine, for several of the older forms of Christianity. This meant that, regardless of what the Bible said on any particular subject, it was the church's view that mattered. They may have gotten this idea from Jesus' words to Peter, about whatever he bound on earth being bound in heaven, and whatever he loosed on earth being loosed in heaven. Some have construed this to mean that Peter (and therefore, in their minds, his successors) could set whatever doctrines and practices they chose, and that God would have to honor them. (They have to ignore much of the rest of the Bible to come to that conclusion, things such as the Bible's statement that God's word is FOREVER SETTLED in heaven, and that not even the smallest part of it would be pass away until all was done. Or the warning Paul gave, and then immediately repeated, to the Galatian church in regard to those who would attempt to alter the original teaching of the apostles in any way: That if even an angel from heaven or an apostle tried to do so, he was to be accursed. Gal. 1:8-9) But since, up until that time, so few had ever even seen a Bible, let alone read one, pretty much nobody knew that it is the word of God that carries the final word, not the church.

What this meant, however, in terms of translation, was this: When the translators encountered portions of scripture that either cast doubt on, or downright contradicted, church teaching, they were of the mindset that the church teaching overruled scripture, and that they were perfectly justified in altering the translation to bring it into line with church teaching. King James had actually given the translators instructions on how to translate, in order to ensure that the new version would conform to the ecclesiology and reflect the episcopal structure of the Church of England and its belief in an ordained clergy.[4] In fact, had they done otherwise, their work would have been rejected from the start: The King James Version was intended to be read from the pulpits of Anglican churches. If it blatantly contradicted Anglican teaching, it could have created problems, questions, and even rebellion. If the translators had presented the King with a Bible that contradicted the teachings of the church, he would have told them to go back and do it over... or perhaps would have replaced those translators with others.

---

[4] Daniell, David. The Bible in English: Its History and Influence, P. 439. New Haven, CT. Yale University Press. 2003.

The goals of the translators themselves aren't above reproach. If one finds an old copy of the King James Version, it may contain a copy of the letter the translators wrote to the King upon completion of their work. Upon reading this letter, it becomes clear that accuracy was not their foremost goal. Their first goal was to flatter the King. The most glaring form of flattery of the King they used was to put his name into the Bible text itself. Some may know that things pertaining to King James are referred to as *Jacobean*. What many don't know is why. The reason why is that the translators of the Bible that bears his name took two men in the New Testament whose name in English should have been Jacob, and renamed them James. James is the anglicized version of the Gaelic *Seamus*, and not at all linguistically connected to Jacob. There is no doubt that James was quite pleased and flattered not only to find his name in the Bible, but even to find an epistle named after him! (Later translators wisely did not change the name back to Jacob. Although it would have been more accurate and honest, it would have resulted in extreme confusion.)

What kind of Bible errors are we talking about? This book deals with a number of them, related to a particular subject. But by no means were those the only errors.

One of the first errors is found in Deuteronomy 6:4. This

verse, known to Jews around the world as the *"sh'ma,"* is, in Hebrew, the ultimate declaration of monotheism, of the absolute Oneness of God. *(Sh'ma* is the first word of the verse in Hebrew, corresponding to the English command *"Hear!")* The KJV renders the verse this way: *"Hear, O Israel, the LORD our God is one LORD."* In English language Old Testaments, LORD in all capital letters represents God's Name, יהוה, often rendered as Jehovah or Yahweh in English. (The original Hebrew form contained only the four consonants, YHVH [sometimes written YHWH], but the vowel sounds were not expressed in writing, thus the actual pronunciation of the name itself is unknown today.) If we read Deut. 6:4 with that understanding, that LORD represents a proper name, we can see readily that the translation makes no sense whatever. Were we to use the same syntax, replacing LORD with another proper name, and God with another position, we can see how inane a statement this is: Hear O Israel, John our mailman is one John. *What is that supposed to mean???*

The problem with the verse for the translators was that, if translated accurately, it made them theologically uncomfortable: "Hear O Israel: YHVH is our God; YHVH is one." While not *technically* incompatible with Anglican doctrine, for those not well versed in the doctrine, it seemed to challenge it. So this verse, as well as the New Testament quote thereof, were "fudged." In fact, any time the text got too close to declaring the original concept of monotheism, the translators seemed to intervene, with only a few exceptions. (There are two definitions of monotheism. The traditional Christian version states only that there is one God. But the original concept, that held by the Jews, also includes the statement that God is one, that is, He exists as one Entity. Traditional Christianity holds a view of the Godhead that is expressed as one God in three Persons. That view is seemingly incompatible with the concept of "God is one." So while the translators were monotheistic from the Christian standpoint of believing in only one God, the statement that God is one made them uncomfortable, as it appeared to challenge the doctrine of three Persons in one God.)

The King James Version, as well as every other English Bible commonly available, begins John's Gospel with two verses stating that the Word was "with God." The Greek text, however, makes no such statement. Literally, the Greek says that the Word was "toward God." Idiomatically, this means "pertained to God." (KJV translated the exact same Greek phrase properly in Heb. 2:17 - "pertaining to God.")

Unfortunately, an entire doctrine, known as the Logos doctrine, has arisen due to this mistranslation. For centuries, people have dissected John 1:1-2, looking for doctrinal statements, when originally, there was no doctrinal statement in those verses. Rather, the first few verses of the Gospel were intended as explanations and definitions. John was writing in Greek, which means his intended audience was the entire Roman Empire, anyone willing to read it. And the overwhelming majority of those people had no idea who the God of Israel was, that He was the only God, etc. It would have been pointless for John to launch right into a narrative about the life and ministry of Jesus when his readers didn't even know who God was. So John sought to identify the God of Israel to his readers.

He had a couple of problems in doing so. Can you imagine trying to introduce someone, but not being able to say the name of the person you were introducing? And that was John's dilemma: He had to introduce the God of Israel, the God of creation, without saying His name. Why? The first reason was custom: Jewish belief held that God's name was so holy that, not only was it not to be uttered aloud, but it was also not to be written down in any language other than Hebrew, the holy language. But even if custom had allowed John to write YHVH in Greek, the Greek alphabet itself would not: It does not have letters necessary to represent all of those consonants. Greek has no letter to represent a consonantal Y. The letter Γ *(gamma) can* sound like a Y, but only if followed by specific vowels. Greek also lacks a letter having the sound of H. It was only possible for that sound to exist at the beginning of a Greek word that started with a vowel, but never in the middle of a word. (Even at the beginning of a word commencing with a vowel, the H sound was not originally represented in writing. And when it was written, centuries later, it was still not with a letter, but an inverted apostrophe.) So John needed to find a way to introduce YHVH without writing His name.

He took a cue from the Aramaic *Targum,* which was the oldest translation of the Tanakh (Old Testament). Following the Jewish people's captivity in Babylon (roughly 597 BC to 537 BC), they no longer used Hebrew in everyday conversation, but used Aramaic instead. Aramaic was the language of Babylon, and its use was imposed on those taken captive by the empire. Over the years of the captivity, the older generation who had grown up speaking Hebrew died, and the younger generation tended to speak Aramaic. Aramaic is closely related to Hebrew, and they share some vocabulary and grammar. And for those Jews returning from captivity, right through the early centuries of the Christian era, Aramaic was even written with the Hebrew alphabet. But when they created an Aramaic version of the *Tanakh* (Old Testament) for everyday use, the translators were reluctant to put God's name in it, even though it was still technically in the Hebrew alphabet. Instead, they replaced it with an Aramaic "codeword." The word they chose was *memra* – ממרא - which means *"word."* (That is, something that is spoken, or in the case of God's name, NOT spoken, aloud.) Readers coming across *memra* would know that it stood for God's name.

John chose the Greek equivalent of *memra*, which was *logos* λόγος. Of course, this word was of no use if his readers didn't know what he meant by it. So in his first few verses, John attempted to explain what he meant by *Logos:*

In the beginning was Logos, and Logos pertained to (meant) God, and Logos was God. This pertained to (meant) God in the beginning. All things were created by Him, and without Him, nothing was made that was made.

From this, his readers would understand that *Logos* referred to the God of creation, the one who made everything in existence, right from the very beginning. And any reader who was familiar with either the *Targum* or the *Septuagint* (Greek Old Testament) would have connected *Logos* with YHVH. None of this was intended to be a doctrinal statement. Not until the 14th verse did John make a doctrinal statement about *Logos:* "And *Logos* became flesh and dwelt among us."

But this statement, read in view of *Logos* being the Creator, was theologically uncomfortable for the translators, so they introduced an artificial division into the Godhead by using the word "with" in verses one and two. (To some believers in the doctrine of the Trinity, it was God the Father who orchestrated creation. So when John said that the Creator became flesh, it sounded like he was saying the Father became the Son, and that teaching is incompatible with trinitarian doctrine.)

In John 8:58, the KJV translators correctly have Jesus saying *"Before Abraham was, I AM."* Inexplicably, however, the next time Jesus made the *I AM* statement, they hid it. This was at His arrest in the garden. Jesus asked the soldiers whom they were seeking. They replied, *"Jesus of Nazareth."* According to KJV, Jesus answered, *"I am he."* But that's not what He said according to the Greek text. What Jesus actually said to them was this: *"I AM."* And what happened next shows us that this was indeed a statement of great power, of His divinity: The moment He said *"I AM,"* those soldiers fell backwards to the ground! (Either He spoke the *I AM* in power, or those were the clumsiest soldiers the world has ever known!)

In Col. 1:19, KJV says *"For it pleased the Father that in him should all fullness dwell."* Other English translations, about half of them, say something similar, some replacing *"the Father"* with *"God."* The problem is that the Greek mentions neither. The Greek says *"For all the fullness was pleased to dwell in Him."* That's a big difference. Paul wrote that the fullness itself was pleased to dwell in Him (Jesus). The translators changed it so that it pleased someone else for the fullness to dwell in Jesus. And yet, again inexplicably, Colossians 2:9, which makes a similar, and even more direct, statement, is rendered correctly: *For in Him dwelleth all the fullness of the Godhead bodily.*

Some who cannot read the original languages may doubt that these errors exist. But the truth is, most of the deliberate errors are so obvious that even a first year student of Hebrew or Greek could spot them. But there is a way to know that there are errors, even if it doesn't resolve them: Go to *biblegateway.com.* Compare a verse in all available English translations. Look at the major discrepancies. That alone tells you that somebody, somewhere, isn't being honest.

For example, compare Deut. 23:17 in all English versions. If we were to believe that all of these translations were correct, we would have to believe that a whore, a prostitute, a shrine prostitute, a temple prostitute, a cult prostitute, a consecrated worker, a ritual harlot, a strumpet, a lecher, a whore-monger, a homosexual and a sodomite all mean exactly the same thing, because those words were all translated from the same two Hebrew words *kadesh* and *kadeshah*. (*Kadesh* and *kadeshah* mean exactly the same thing, but one is male, the other female, like actor/actress or waiter/waitress.) Obviously, while some of those terms are synonymous (shrine prostitute = cult prostitute = temple prostitute), the others don't fit at all. Temple prostitution was a form of worship of the goddess of fertility, and bore little in common with ordinary prostitution. (An ordinary prostitute, in Hebrew, is a *zonah*. That word is found in Deut. 23:18.) And a prostitute, a lecher, a whore-monger and a homosexual aren't even remotely synonymous. And as for sodomite, we won't address that here. It's addressed in the chapter on Sodom. But suffice it to say that there is no such word as sodomite in the Hebrew or Greek texts of scripture. Greek had no such word at all, so far as we know. Hebrew *has* such a word, but it is not found at all in the Bible. The Hebrew form, *s'domi,* as a noun, has only ONE meaning: *a person from Sodom.*

In light of the indisputable fact that our Bibles contain numerous errors in translation, many of them deliberate, the advice of Paul to Timothy takes on a whole new meaning:

Study to show yourself approved to God, a worker who does not need to be ashamed, correctly dividing the word of truth. (2 Tim. 2:15)

This HAS to entail more than memorizing verses from a favorite translation and simply assuming that they have been correctly translated into English. Today, there are sufficient tools available online for anyone, even with no prior knowledge of Hebrew and Greek, to begin to learn to read those languages. And copies of the Hebrew and Greek texts themselves are freely available online. The resources to "study" are there, at our disposal, giving us a tremendous advantage over Christians of prior centuries to whom scripture was either unavailable or available only in an obscure, dead language. Everything we need to know the truth is at our fingertips. *"And you shall know the truth, and the truth shall make you free."*

Adam and Eve vs. Adam and Steve

One argument used against homosexuality suggests that because the first couple was heterosexual, then all future couples were also intended to be heterosexual.

But let's look again at our first parents, Adam and Eve. A lot of what we have been taught about them, about the garden, about the fall, is based more upon tradition and medieval paintings than on scripture. (How many know that the Bible never said the fruit they ate was an apple?) A careful reading of the Hebrew text will reveal some surprising things about this couple to us.

The scripture tells us that God made man out of the dust of the ground. This first man is known to us as Adam, but Adam was not originally a proper name. Adam, more properly spelled with a small "a," is nothing more than the Hebrew word for human being. So God created *adam* אדם (ah-DAHM), a human being, out of dust. The human being was placed in the garden of Eden. Also in the garden were the animals God created, and the human being gave them all names. The world order was different at that time: Because there was no sin, there was no death, and because there was no death, there was no need for any procreation. (If the animals had been reproducing in an enclosed garden, and nothing ever died, there would soon have been massive overpopulation.) The man also gave a name to himself, different from the word *adam* that God had called him. He called himself אנוש *"enosh."* This wasn't exactly a proper name either, but meant *man*. (*Enosh* is the oldest form of the word. In biblical and modern Hebrew, this word has become איש *"ish."*) Proper names were not needed due to the fact that there was only one of him, and only a limited number of animals. (If there was only one tiger, one tigress, one lion, one lioness, etc., they could be called by those names; other names were not needed.)

It was that pairing of all the other creatures that caused the man his first "problem." The lion had a lioness that he could recognize as being "like him." The tigress had the tiger, etc. But although there are many species that look like man, there was no other creature in the garden that *enosh* could recognize as being like him. In that respect, he was alone.

God said that it was not good for the *adam* to be alone (Gen. 2:18) and went on to say *"I will make a help meet for him."* (King James Version) But what the Hebrew says here, and the manner in which God made this "help," tell us volumes about the creature He was about to present to the man. The words translated as "help meet" are עזר כנגדו *E-zer k'NEG-do*. The word עזר *"ezer"* means *"helper."* But there is more to it than that: Hebrew has no neuter gender; every word is either masculine or feminine. Nouns referring to people usually have both a masculine form and a feminine form, like "actor" and "actress" in English. *Ezer* is masculine. The feminine form would be עזרה *ezrah*. But God didn't say He would make an *ezrah*. He used the masculine form, *ezer*. The second half of this, כנגדו *k'negdo,* means "as opposite him," that is, as a mirror image.

The way in which God created this helper is also significant. He could easily have taken some of the same dust from which He made the *adam*, and formed the helper out of it. Instead, we find that He took a rib from the man and made the woman from it. This is very significant. From what we now know about genetics, we can understand what God did: Although it sounds frightening to say it, the plain fact is, God cloned another *adam* from the rib. Because the new *adam* was made from the first *adam's* DNA, the two had to be genetically identical in every way. (Was Eve also called Adam? In Genesis 1:27, the Hebrew tells us that *adam* was made both male and female. Genesis 5:1-2 tells us the same thing, and that **their** name was called *adam*.) When God made this new person, the first *adam* called her אנשה *"inshah,"* which is simply the feminine form of *enosh*. It means "woman." (Biblical and modern Hebrew: אשה *ishah*) But we know from modern cloning experiments that a clone cannot have a different sex than the original. Therefore, the woman would have actually been no different from the man. (Remember that there was no need for reproduction yet.) The response of the man when he met the woman for the first time confirms this. When the *adam* saw his new helper for the first time (and remember, he had never before seen a human female), he did not say *"What are those things?"* or *"Why is she missing the parts below?"* If there were a physical difference, he would have noticed it immediately. Instead, he recognized her as *"bone of my bones and flesh of my flesh."* He knew that she was his counterpart, his mirror image. He gave her the feminine equivalent of his name for himself.

The need for procreation came about as a result of the fall. Because of sin, there was now death, and with expulsion from the garden, there was a whole world to fill. All of creation now needed to reproduce. Having children was part of the curse placed on the woman. Translating from the Hebrew, God told her, *"I will surely multiply your sorrow and pregnancy: In sorrow you will bear children, and your desire will be toward your man* (literally, *toward your enosh), and he will rule over you."* So we see that pregnancy, bringing forth children, was not part of her original state, but was part of the curse. So if childbearing were not part of her original design, then she would not originally have needed those parts of the body associated with bearing and nursing children. (It is also probable that her husband lacked parts associated with reproduction prior to the fall as well.) What is clear is this: Prior to their sin and expulsion, the man and woman were alike, equal, and appeared to have no physical differences from each other. Their DNA was identical. They were not heterosexual in the modern sense of the word, because there was no sexuality of any kind, nor any difference between sexes. In fact, the only difference evident in scripture before the fall was grammatical: They were both *adam*, but he was *enosh*, she was *inshah*. The difference served only to point out which *adam* was being spoken of. (For example, a lion and lioness: if they were originally physically identical, the different titles would serve only to indicate which big cat you were speaking of, and would not reflect any physical difference.)

After the fall, when the changes took place, *enosh* gave his helper a new name. (These changes included diet: Before the fall, no animal ate another. Much of creation had to be redesigned so that humans and animals, all originally designed as herbivores, could now chew and digest meat.) When *enosh* realized that *inshah* would be bearing children, he gave her a name that reflected her new status: He called her Chavah (Hebrew: חוה – *"living"*), or Eve in English, because she would be the mother of all the living. So we see that prior to the fall, she was not a mother, she was not Eve, and physically, she was not even female as we understand the word. So one of the first consequences of sin that came into being was heterosexuality, required to replace those humans and animals who died. But in addition, homosexuality came into being, to prevent overpopulation in the world. A percentage of many hundreds of animal species are homosexual.[5] Although it was sin that brought this into being, it was nevertheless God who designed the new order that resulted from our sin. His new order for creation included sexuality, absent from the garden, and included the orientations we know today.

---

[5] Bagemihl, Ph.D., Bruce. "Biological Exuberance: Animal Homosexuality and Natural Diversity." New York. St. Martin's Press. 2000.

QUESTION: Wasn't the command to *"Be fruitful, and multiply, and replenish the earth"* (Gen. 1:28) given before the fall?

ANSWER: No. It is important to understand that the first chapter of Genesis is an *overview* of all creation, a *synopsis*, and includes events from both *before* the fall and *after* the fall. Chapter two then goes back and tells the story of the creation of man again, in more detail, including the specifics of the fall and the expulsion from the garden.

So how do we know which events in chapter one were after the fall? Simple logic: Prior to the fall, man and the animals were in the garden, a space enclosed by four rivers. This brings up two important points:

1. In the absence of death, it would make no sense at all for God to command anyone or anything to reproduce in an enclosed space. The rats and rabbits alone would have overrun the place in a matter of months, if not weeks!

2. Notice that the command given to man was to *"replenish the earth."* (Better translation: *"fill the earth."*) But prior to the fall, man was in the garden and didn't have access to the whole earth, so they could not possibly fill it! Clearly this command was given *after* the fall.

The Sin of Sodom Wasn't What You Think

One of the more common arguments against homosexuality used to be the destruction of Sodom and Gomorrah. We say "used to be," because many biblical scholars and teachers today realize that there is no scriptural backing for that argument. Let us together take a clear, honest look at these cities, and let us determine who the inhabitants were, and why God destroyed them.

The first thing to realize is that it wasn't just two cities involved. Today, people usually only remember the names of two, but in truth, God was about to destroy all the cities of the plain. In addition to Sodom and Gomorrah, the cities of Admah, Zeboiim and Zoar were also about to be destroyed. (Gen. 14:2; Deut. 29:23) Zoar was spared so that Lot and his daughters could flee there, but Admah and Zeboiim met the same fate as Sodom and Gomorrah. Another interesting point is that, at least in reference to Sodom, Gomorrah and Zoar, the Bible doesn't tell us their real names. The Hebrew word for Sodom is סדם *S'dom* and means "burnt." The Hebrew word for Gomorrah is עמורה *'Amorah,* and means "a ruined heap." Zoar צער *Tso'ar* means "insignificance." (Lot pointed out that it was a small, insignificant city when asking the angels if he and his daughters could go there and be safe.) There can be no question that these names were given to the cities *after* they were destroyed, and were not their original names.

The inhabitants of these cities, like all the Canaanites, were worshippers of false gods. These included the god Molech, arguably the most horrible of all the idols of Canaan. According to the writing of the rabbinical scholar Rashi, Molech was a huge statue with his arms held out in front of him. A fire would be kindled between his arms, and then babies would be placed in his arms and burned alive. This was known as "passing your children through the fire to Molech."

Other practices engaged in by the Canaanites included adult human sacrifice, cannibalism (Wisdom of Solomon 12:5), and temple prostitution. (Having sexual relations with temple prostitutes as a form of worship in fertility cults.)

Lot, Abraham's nephew, moved to the city of Sodom with

his wife and their daughters. God sent two angels to Sodom in the evening, ostensibly to investigate the rumors of the sinfulness of the city, i.e., so they could experience first hand what was going on there. A more important purpose of their visit, though, (since God obviously already knew what was going on) was to rescue Lot and his family from the impending destruction. The account of their visit to the city is found in Genesis 19. Lot was sitting in the gate. This is significant. The person who sat in the gate, that is, the gatekeeper, was entrusted by the rulers of the city to monitor all traffic in and out of the city, and not to admit anyone who could endanger the city in any way. This was a serious responsibility, and the fact that it was given to Lot, who was not a native of the city, but a relative newcomer, was unusual.

A word about the angels: Forget, for a moment, the traditional stereotypes of angels, that is, women with flowing blond hair and huge feathered wings. In scripture, angels usually appeared in the form of men. Frequently, there was nothing unusual about their appearance that would suggest they were anything other than human beings.

Lot greeted the two visitors, as was his responsibility as gatekeeper. (He bowed to the ground, which was not an uncommon form of greeting from an inferior to a superior, in this case, from a public servant to strangers whose social status was unknown.) He then evidently inquired about their business in the city and specific destination, again, as part of his job. Upon learning that they intended to spend the night in the street, Lot insisted that they stay at his house. This suggests he knew they would not be safe in the streets. The obvious aside, that there has probably never been a city where it is safe to sleep in the streets at night, the reason for Lot's insistence becomes clear when we read certain passages in the *Mishnah*, which is pre-Christian Jewish Bible commentary. Those texts contain detailed information on the situation in Sodom that led to its demise.

According to the *Mishnah*, Sodom was unfathomably cruel to strangers and the poor. For example, a visitor to Sodom would be offered a bed for the night... but if the bed were too long or short for the visitor, it was the visitor they altered: A person who was too short would be stretched on a rack until he fit the bed. Someone who was too tall would have his feet and enough of his legs amputated, until he fit the bed.[6]

In regard to the poor, the people of Sodom were happy to offer a coin or two to a beggar. But the coins they offered had a mark on them... and no merchant in town would accept those coins in payment for anything. When the poor beggar

---

[6] Talmud, Sanhedrin 109a

finally starved to death, the coins would be reclaimed, and would be given to other poor people.[7]

Once the people of Sodom had found out that P'lotit, Lot's daughter, had secretly given food to a stranger who was near starvation, and they burned her in public. Another time, when they discovered that a teenage girl had fed a starving beggar, they smeared honey all over her and placed her upon the city wall, so that she died from the stings of the bees and/or wasps attracted by the honey.[8] Some traditions hold that it was the "cry" of the young girl hung from the walls which reached God. This was the "cry" of which He spoke to Abraham, and which ultimately led to the destruction of Sodom and the other cities. Behavior like this would most certainly qualify as grievous. ***"Because the cry of Sodom and Gomorrah is great, and because their sin is very grievous."*** (Gen. 18:20)

These and many other similar hideous acts of cruelty by the people of Sodom and the other cities had aroused God's anger, and He decided to destroy them completely.

Understanding, then, how the people of Sodom treated visitors to their city, it can readily be understood why Lot was so insistent that the two men not stay in the streets, and why he urgently propelled them toward his own house for the

---

[7] Talmud, Sanhedrin 109b

[8] Isaacs, Jacob. "Our People." Brooklyn, NY. Kehot Publication Society. 1946.

night.

Lot did insist, and the two visitors went to his house and he made dinner for them. Later that night, a mob formed outside of Lot's house, demanding that he bring out the guests. Traditionalists would have us believe that the mob was made up of homosexual men wanting to have sex with the angels. But a careful reading of the verses shows clearly that this was not the case. Gen. 19:4 tells us *"But before they lay down, the men of the city, even the men of Sodom, compassed the house round, both old and young, all the people from every quarter."* At first glance, it does appear to be a crowd of men. But let's look deeper. The phrase *"the men of the city, even the men of Sodom"* is a bit misleading. In Hebrew, אנשי העיר אנשי סדם *"anshei ha'ir, anshei S'dom,"* could also be translated as *"the people of the city, the people of Sodom."* But is that a more correct translation? The rest of the verse will answer that for us: *"...both old and young, **all the people** from every quarter."* There is no question, then, that the entire population of Sodom gathered outside Lot's house: men, women and children. This alone tells us that the traditionalists were wrong about the intent of the mob: If you are planning a homosexual orgy, you don't invite the wife and kids!

Of course, this begs the question, how did this mob come to form, and what did they really want? The Bible doesn't tell us, so we have to read between the lines and in so doing, backtrack from the mob scene outside Lot's house to where the crowd first gathered. First, the fact that the entire population of the city was involved tells us that this was, to them, a matter of some importance. They evidently felt that the visit of these two strangers was something that affected every person in the city in some way. So logic suggests that the gathering would have begun at whatever public place Sodom used for such things, such as a City Hall or public square or the King's palace. Here was the situation as they would have seen it: Lot, a foreigner who had moved here and had been given a position of some responsibility, had invited two strangers of unknown origin into the city and into his home. But his job as gatekeeper did not include sneaking strangers into the city. Sodom had an established way of dealing with visitors to the city, as horrible as that way was. So the crowd devised a plan: They would go to Lot's house and politely ask to meet the strangers and know who they were. They even had their words chosen: *"Where are the men who came to you tonight? Bring them out and let us know them."* It should be noted that this was phrased as a request, using a polite form of the verb *"to know,"*[9] and was not phrased in a hostile, demanding way. And so the crowd began to move toward Lot's house.

There are those who claim that when the crowd said *"let us know them,"* they meant *"have sex with them."* There are even translations of the Bible that say *"let us have sex with them,"* or *"let us know them carnally."* Let us state categorically, that the Hebrew text will NOT support such "translations."

Some would say that Hebrew has more than one verb for *"know,"* and that the one used here means *"have sex."* Let's set the record straight on this: There is no separate Hebrew verb that means "know" in a sexual sense. The root of the Hebrew verb for *"know"* is ידע *yada*. A form of *yada* is used here and hundreds of other times in scripture. Only about ten of those times refer to sex, and in each case, the sexual meaning is made clear by the immediate context. (Example: *Adam knew his wife and she conceived.*) To try to make this word mean sex everywhere will get us in a lot of trouble, because the scripture tells us that God knew David, and uses a form of this word. We don't think anyone would be foolish enough to try to attach a sexual meaning to that. When the crowd outside Lot's house said they wanted to know the

---

[9]Adding the letter ה to the end of a future tense verb changes it from an ordinary future to a polite request. נדע = we will know; נדעה = let us know.

visitors, they meant exactly that: To know who they were. Of course, given their history in regard to visitors, it wasn't likely to end with them learning the identity of the men, and Lot knew that.

Even though the crowd assembled more or less peacefully, and delivered a polite request to know the identity of his guests, Lot knew that wasn't the end of it. He had lived in that city long enough to know what they did to overnight guests. His guests might not survive having their feet and part of their legs violently amputated. And being stretched on a rack could leave them permanently crippled. Lot couldn't allow that.

There was, at the time, an unwritten "law of hospitality," something Lot undoubtedly had learned from his uncle Abraham. That law stated that if visitors came to your home, you were responsible not only to feed and house them, but also to protect them, even at the cost of your own life and the lives of your family. So Lot took his responsibility very seriously, and wasn't about to turn his guests over to the crowd.

Of course, a tiny family like Lot's couldn't hope to fight off such a mob. The only hope in such cases is to try to talk them out of it, or, failing in that, to try to distract them in some way. Lot tried both. He went out to them and asked them not to behave so wickedly. The hostile intentions of the mob were clear to him, despite the polite words they used. It was also clear immediately that talking was not going to work. In fact, his attempts to dissuade them only served to enrage them.

Lot, in desperation to protect his visitors, did what the law of hospitality required: He was willing to sacrifice the lives of his daughters to protect the guests. A word about the two daughters: These girls were engaged to two men from Sodom. An engagement was much more binding in those days than it is today. In fact, it was as binding as a marriage, and even gave Lot some authority over his daughters' fiancés. Lot offered his two daughters, still virgins, to the crowd in place of the strangers. If he could distract the men of the crowd, then they, as the leaders of the city, might have disbanded the mob, or at least have been distracted long enough that he could get his guests out of the city to safety.

Think about this: If the men of Sodom had been homosexual and wanted sex with his guests, there is no way Lot would not have known. He would have known it would be pointless to offer women to homosexual men. He could, and would, have offered them something they would be more likely to accept: He could have offered his future sons-in-law, since the engagement of his daughters gave him that right, or, he could even have offered himself. But if the crowd outside Lot's house really had been interested in raping the men inside, though, it hardly seems plausible that they would politely ask permission to do so, using a mild euphemism for sex. A rape gang would be far more likely to use crude and vulgar language. *Rapists don't ask permission, and they don't use mild euphemisms for sex!*

Lot's offer was refused, and the crowd seized him, and said they were going to do worse to him than they were planning to do to his guests. Did they attempt any type of sexual contact with Lot? No, they tried to kill him.[10] There was no sexual situation here at all. But, just for the sake of argument, if the intent of the crowd had been to force the angels to have sex, their crime would have been rape, not homosexuality.

It also bears mentioning that whatever happened, or did not happen, at Lot's house had no bearing on the destruction of Sodom or the other cities. Their fate had been sealed before those angels ever came to the city.

Ezekiel recorded the sins of Sodom: Ezek. 16:49-50 - pride, fullness of bread, and abundance of idleness. They did not strengthen the hand of the poor and needy, they were haughty and committed abomination. A note about this

---

[10] Gen. 19:9 ויפצרו באיש בלוט מאד – "and they pushed the man Lot extremely."

unspecified abomination: In the Law of Moses, many things were called abomination, including such things as eating pork and shellfish, having sex with a woman during her period, etc. But the word abomination simply means "a hateful thing."[11] Certainly, the way Sodom and the other cities treated the poor and strangers to the cities, and even their own people, was a hateful thing. Outside the Law of Moses, the word abomination was often used to refer to practices associated with idol worship, some of which were enumerated earlier. And as mentioned earlier, the *Mishnah* is clear that Sodom was destroyed because of their cruelty to strangers and the poor. There is no suggestion there that homosexual activity was a factor. In fact, historically, the first religious text to suggest such a thing was the Quran (c. AD 600).[12]

What about sodomites? In modern times, the word sodomy was incorporated into many states' laws in the U.S. But it did not mean the same thing in each state. In some states, sodomy referred only to anal intercourse. In other states, it also included homosexual oral sex, and in some states, it even included heterosexual oral sex. For some, anything other than heterosexual vaginal intercourse was

---

[11] תועבה – to'evah – a hateful thing

[12] Quran 54:37

sodomy.[1314] These definitions all go back to the incorrect notion that Sodom was destroyed for "unnatural" sexual activity. As we have seen above, that simply wasn't the case.

But what about biblical references to sodomites? In the King James Version, this word can be found in a few places, including Deut. 23:17 and 2 Kings 23:7. In some translations, the word is even found in the New Testament. But if we look at the Hebrew Old Testament and the Greek New Testament, that is, if we look at the Bible in its original languages, we will never see such a word as sodomite in there. So when we see it in an English translation, we must acknowledge that the translators lied.

Let us look at the above two verses in more detail: In the King James Version, Deuteronomy 23:17 tells us that there will not be a "whore" of the daughters of Israel, nor a "sodomite" of the sons of Israel. Now, if we look at the verse in the Hebrew text, it tells us that there will not be a קדשה *kadeshah* of the daughters of Israel nor a קדש *kadesh* of the sons of Israel. Even if you don't know a word of Hebrew, you can see that the words are very similar. In fact, *kadeshah* is simply the feminine form of *kadesh*, so whatever it is that the

---

[13]Phelps, Shirelle. "World of Criminal Justice: N-Z." p. 686. Farmington Hills, MI. Gale Group. 2001.

[14]Scheb, John, John Scheb, II. "Criminal Law and Procedure." p. 185. Boston. Cengage Learning. 2013.

daughters were not to be, is *exactly* the same as what the sons were not to be. So which is it, whore, or sodomite? Actually, neither. A *kadeshah* is not a prostitute in the usual sense, that is, not a "street hostess" who plies her living by having sex for money. Rather, *kadesh* and *kadeshah* were **temple** prostitutes. These were a feature of Babylonian, and later Canaanite, fertility religions. The temple prostitutes usually lived in or near the temple, and having sex with one of them was a form of worship of the goddess of fertility. The money paid was put in the temple treasury, rather than given to the prostitute. It should be noted that both men and women would visit the temple prostitutes to "worship" in this way. It should also be noted that because this was part of a fertility cult, temple prostitution was ALWAYS heterosexual. Israel ignored the prohibition of temple prostitution fairly early in their history. In 1 Samuel 2:22, we read that the two sons of Eli the High Priest, Hophni and Phineas, who were themselves priests, were having sex with the women of Israel in the doorway of the Tabernacle. (This public location proves this was temple prostitution, and not just the two men cheating on their wives).

Let's look now at 2 Kings 23:7. The translation in the King James refers to sodomites again, but also has errors in other parts of the translation, so the verse is reproduced here translated directly from the Hebrew text: "And he broke down the houses of the temple prostitutes (Hebrew: קְדֵשִׁים *kadeshim*) that were in the house of the LORD, where the women wove houses (i.e., shrines) for Asherah." *(Note: Asherah was one of the names given by the Canaanites to the Babylonian fertility goddess.)*

One final thought about the cities of the plain, that is, Sodom, etc.: Jude 7 talks about the people of these cities giving themselves over to fornication (definition: any sexual activity outside of marriage, including temple prostitution) and *"going after strange flesh."* (King James Version). What does that last part mean? The truth is, no one can say for sure. But the translation isn't correct. The Greek does not say *"strange flesh,"* but rather *"other flesh."* The word for *other* is ἑτέρας *"heteras"*. Exactly what the phrase means is uncertain. But given the fact that the word translated as *flesh* is also the word for *meat*, it is quite possible that it is referring to the practices of cannibalism associated with early Canaanite culture.

Leviticus 18:22

The translation of this verse found in English versions is wrong. Below, we have presented the verse, and will take it apart word by word to show what it actually says.

וְאֶת־זָכָר לֹא תִשְׁכַּב מִשְׁכְּבֵי אִשָּׁה תּוֹעֵבָה הִוא:

V'et-zachar lo tishkav mishkvei ishah to'evah hu:

(Transliterated using modern Israeli Sephardic pronunciation.)

וְאֶת[15] *V'et* - This is two words. First, וְ *V'*, which means *and*. This word cannot exist by itself, and therefore is attached to the word that comes after it, that is, אֶת *et*. This word means *with*. So the first two words of this verse are *And with*.

זָכָר *zachar* - This word means *male*. Hebrew has no indefinite article (a, an), so when the definite article (the) is not used, as in this case, an indefinite article is understood for purposes of translation. Therefore, this word translates as *a male*. The verse so far reads *And with a male*.

---
[15] Hebrew is written and read from right to left, the opposite of English.

לֹא *lo* - This word is the Hebrew equivalent of our words *no* and *not*. It is used in this case to negate the verb that follows it. Because English has a more complicated verb structure than Hebrew, it will take more than one English word to translate the next Hebrew word, and the *not* will need to go in the middle of those words, so we won't add this word to our translation yet.

תשכב *tishkav* - This is a verb. Unlike English verbs, everything we need to know about tense and person is contained in this one word. No additional pronouns or tense markers are needed. The root of the verb is the last three letters: שכב *sh-k-v*, and it means *lie down*. The first letter of the word, ת *t*, is not part of the root, but indicates person and tense and even gender. To translate *tishkav* into English will require four words, as well as a parenthetical note to indicate the gender of the pronoun. The word translates as *Thou (masculine, that is, speaking to a male) shalt lie down*. The previous Hebrew word, לֹא *lo*, negated the verb, so we have *And with a male thou shalt not lie down*.

משכבי *mishk'vei* - This is a noun. The base form of the noun is משכב *mishkav*, and it can be seen that the last three letters of the base, שכב sh-k-v, are also the three letters of the verb root above, meaning *lie down*. This noun means *bed*. Hebrew nouns have more than one form. In addition to having singular and plural forms, many nouns also have absolute and construct forms. An absolute noun stands alone, with its own meaning. A construct noun is grammatically tied to the noun that follows it. In translating to English, this usually involves placing the English word *"of"* between the two nouns. A good example is the Hebrew בית־לחם *Beit Lechem* (Bethlehem), which in English translates as *House of Bread*. This is because the first word, בית *Beit*, is in the construct state. *Mishk'vei* is in the construct state, meaning *bed of*.[16] It would be a good idea to explain a bit about Hebrew prepositions now: Hebrew *has* prepositions that correspond to ours, but doesn't always *use* them the same way. For example, when people leave us, in English we will say that *we miss them*. But in Hebrew, the verb *to miss* is used with a preposition, and we say that *we miss **to** them*. The same works in reverse, that is, sometimes English requires a preposition when Hebrew doesn't. If a preposition can be derived from context, Hebrew will sometimes leave it out. In English, we nearly always need it. Therefore, we need to

---

[16]Technically, "beds of," as it is plural. But in Hebrew, use of a plural noun does not necessarily imply more than one. It can be used to emphasize importance.

insert the English word *in* before the words *bed of,* in order for the sentence to make sense in English. The verse so far reads *And with a male thou shalt not lie down in bed of.*

אשה *ishah* - This is the Hebrew word for *woman*. Since there is no definite article (the), it is understood to mean *a woman*. *And with a male thou shalt not lie down in bed of a woman.* Since *bed of a woman* is awkward in English, we would use our possessive case, and say *"a woman's bed."* *And with a male thou shalt not lie down in a woman's bed.*

Punctuation as we know it was not part of the original text. Even modern Hebrew Bibles contain only one punctuation mark, which looks like a colon ':', but serves only to point out the end of a verse (but not necessarily the end of a sentence). English is very difficult to read without punctuation marks, so we insert them as we translate. After the word woman, we may insert either a semicolon, or a period, to indicate that the following words are not part of the first phrase, but simply offer further information about it. *And with a male thou shalt not lie down in a woman's bed;*

תועבה *to'evah* - This is a noun. It translates as *abomination (i.e. "a hateful thing")*. Without a definite article, it translates as *an abomination*. Hebrew word order often varies from ours, and this is one case where this is true. In English, this will be the *last* word in the sentence, so we will hold off on adding it to the translation until we have finished with the next word.

הוּא *hu* - This little word serves so many purposes, not only for readers of the Hebrew text, but also for those today who wonder about the accuracy of the Hebrew text. You see, this word is a grammatical error made by Moses.[17] Moses was well schooled in the arts and sciences of ancient Egypt, but not in the tongue of his own people. Although he evidently spoke Hebrew well enough to be understood, like so many today, he did not always use proper grammar. His meaning remained the same, but the grammar was wrong. Let's say that again: **His meaning remained the same, only the grammar was wrong.** The word הוּא *hu* means both *he* and *it*. It means *it* when applied to masculine nouns. But *to'evah* is a feminine noun, so Moses should have used the word היא *hi*, which means *she* and *it*. It means *it* when applied to feminine nouns. (All Hebrew nouns are either masculine or

---

[17] There are some today who do not believe Moses wrote the Torah or Pentateuch (first five books of the Old Testament). They were historically attributed to him, and this author does believe he wrote them.

feminine; Hebrew has no neuter gender. This gender concept is grammatical in nature only, and has nothing to do with men or women, per se. For example, in Hebrew a table is masculine, whereas in the Romance languages, it is feminine. It has nothing to do with the nature of the table; it's simply grammatical.)

So what does Moses' error do for us? It doesn't change the meaning, as we mentioned above. It still means *it*. But the significant thing is that the error has never been corrected. Why? Didn't anyone notice it? Of course, they did. But the Jewish people consider the text of the Hebrew Bible so sacred, that they will not alter even simple grammatical errors. The Jewish people considered even the shapes of the letters of the alphabet to be holy. The most they could do about the error was point it out, without correcting it. They did this by using the vowel point for the correct word with the incorrect word: הִוא The resulting word is more or less unpronounceable, but serves to alert the reader to the error. (The Hebrew alphabet itself has no vowels, only consonants. The reader was expected to be able to supply the vowel sounds from context, etc. By the early medieval period, Hebrew was developing dialects, partially due to the fact that there were no vowels to tell people how to pronounce it. The Rabbis and scholars devised a system of dots and dashes to represent vowels and alterations to consonant sounds. These vowel "points" are placed inside, above, below and next to letters, but may not touch the letters. They are not considered part of the text. Today they are used in Bibles, prayer books, song and poetry books, and children's books, but are rarely used in newspapers, novels, etc.) *And with a male thou shalt not lie down in a woman's bed; it*

Our next point of grammar involves the present tense forms of the verb *to be*. In English these forms are *am, art, is* and *are*. Hebrew *has* such forms,[18] but almost never uses them, except in reference to God, or when absolutely necessary for context. The reason for this may be that the forms are too close to God's name in Hebrew. While this may seem awkward to us, there are many other languages that don't use the present tense of the verb *to be*. For example, Russian has become so used to ignoring the forms, that some of them are completely obsolete. (The Russian equivalent of *am* [есмь] can't even be found in a dictionary or grammar book anymore.) They get along fine without those forms, and so does Hebrew. But English can't, so we have to insert the appropriate forms when translating: *And with a male thou*

---

[18] הווה hoveh, הווה hovah, הווים hovim, הוות hovot

shalt not lie down in a woman's bed; it is

Finally, we put in the words *an abomination*: *And with a male thou shalt not lie down in a woman's bed; it is an abomination.* This is the correct translation of Leviticus 18:22. It can be seen that, rather than forbidding male homosexuality, it simply forbids two males to lie down in a woman's bed, for whatever reason. Culturally, a woman's bed was her own. Other than the woman herself, only her husband was permitted in her bed, and there were even restrictions on when he was allowed in there. Any other use of her bed would have been considered defilement. Other verses in the Law will help clarify the acceptable use of the woman's bed (Lev. 15).

Leviticus 20:13

(Note: Some of the material in this chapter is identical to the previous chapter, due to the similarities between this verse and Lev. 18:22.)

ואיש אשר ישכב את־זכר משכבי אשה תועבה עשו שניהם מות יומתו דמיהם בם:

V'ish asher yishkav et-zachar mishk'vei ishah to'evah asu shneihem mot yumatu d'meihem bam.

(Transliterated using modern Israeli Sephardic pronunciation.)

ואיש *V'ish* - This is two words. First, **ו** *V'*, which means *and*. This word cannot exist by itself, and therefore is attached to the word that comes after it, that is, **איש** *ish*. This word means *man*. Hebrew has no indefinite article (a, an), so when the definite article (the) is not used, as in this case, an indefinite article is understood. Therefore, this word translates as *a man*. So the first two words of this verse are *And a man*.

אשר *asher* - This word is a relative pronoun, meaning *who, which* or *that*, depending on context. Since it is used with *a man*, it would mean *who*. *And a man who*.

ישכב *yishkav* - This is a verb. Unlike English verbs, everything we need to know about tense and person is contained in this one word. No additional pronouns or tense markers are needed. The root of the verb is the last three letters: שכב *sh-k-v*, and it means *lie down*. The first letter of the word, י *y*, is not part of the root, but indicates person and tense and even gender. To translate *yishkav* into English will require four words. The word translates as *he will lie down*. If a subject is already present in the sentence, as in this case, then the pronoun of the verb (he) is omitted in translation. *And a man who will lie down*.

את *et* - This word means *with*. *And a man who will lie down with*.

זכר *zachar* - This word means *(a) male*. The verse so far

reads *And a man who will lie down with a male*.

מִשְׁכְּבֵי *mishk'vei* - This is a noun. The base form of the noun is מִשְׁכָּב *mishkav*, and it can be seen that the last three letters of the base, שׁכב *sh-k-v*, are also the three letters of the verb root above, meaning *lie down*. This noun means *bed*. Hebrew nouns have more than one form. In addition to having singular and plural forms, many nouns also have absolute and construct forms. An absolute noun stands alone, with its own meaning. A construct noun is grammatically tied to the noun that follows it. In translating to English, this usually involves placing the English word *"of"* between the two nouns. A good example is the Hebrew בֵּית־לֶחֶם *Beit Lechem* (Bethlehem), which in English translates as *House of Bread*. This is because the first word, בֵּית *Beit*, is in the construct state. *Mishk'vei* is in the construct state, meaning *bed of*.[19] It would be a good idea here to explain a bit about Hebrew prepositions: Hebrew *has* prepositions that correspond to ours, but doesn't always *use* them the same way. For example, when people leave us, in English we say that *we miss them*. But in Hebrew, the verb *to miss* is used

---

[19]Technically, "beds of," as it is plural. But in Hebrew, use of a plural noun does not necessarily imply more than one. It can be used to emphasize importance.

with a preposition, and we say that *we miss **to** them*. The same works in reverse, that is, sometimes English requires a preposition when Hebrew doesn't. If a preposition can be derived from context, Hebrew will sometimes leave it out. In English, we nearly always need it. Therefore, we need to insert the English word *in* before the words *bed of* in order for the sentence to make sense in English. The verse so far reads *And a man who will lie down with a male in bed of.*

אשה *ishah* - This is the Hebrew word for *woman*. Since there is no definite article (the), it is understood to mean *a woman*. *And a man who will lie down with a male in bed of a woman.* Since *bed of a woman* is awkward in English, we would use our possessive case, and say *"a woman's bed."* *And with a male thou shalt not lie down in a woman's bed.*

תועבה *to'evah* - This is a noun. It translates as *abomination*. (i.e., a hateful thing) Without a definite article, it translates as *an abomination*. Hebrew word order often varies from ours, and this is one case where this is true. In English, this word will come later in the sentence, so we will hold off on adding it to the translation until we have finished with the next two words.

עשו *asu* - This is a verb. It means *make* or *do*. This form is past tense, and translates as *they have made* or *they have done*. A subject for the verb is following in the sentence, so the word *they* can be left out of the translation. In English, word order is usually subject-verb-object, so in order for our translation to make sense, the next word, which is the subject, will need to come before this word and the previous word.

שניהם *shneihem* - This word is made of two particles combined. First is שני *shnei*, which is the construct form of the number *two*. Because it is construct, we add the English word *of* to the translation: *Two of*. The second particle is הם *hem*, which is called a pronominal ending. Depending on context, it translates as *they, them* or *their* (all masculine). Put together, this word means *two of them*, or less awkwardly, *both of them. And a man who will lie down with a male in a woman's bed, both of them have done an abomination;*

מות *mot* - This is a gerund form of the verb *to die*. It corresponds to our word *dying. And a man who will lie down with a male in a woman's bed, both of them have done an abomination; dying.*

יוּמָתוּ *yumatu* - This is a future form of a different paradigm of the same verb. It translates as *they will be put to death*. The phrase *dying they will be put to death* expresses the certainty of the sentence, and is rendered in some English versions as *they will surely die,* which is an acceptable rendering. *And a man who will lie down with a male in a woman's bed, both of them have done an abomination; dying they will be put to death,*

דְּמֵיהֶם *d'meihem* - This word is made of two particles combined. The first is דְּמֵי *d'mei,* a construct form of the word for *blood*. Because it is construct, we *could* insert *of* after it, but we will see further on that adding *of* in this case would make the translation awkward. The second particle is the pronominal ending הֶם *hem*, as seen above in *shneihem*. Put together, this word means *blood of them*. Since this is awkward, we would translate the word as *their blood. And a man who will lie down with a male in a woman's bed, both of them have done an abomination; dying they will be put to death, their blood.*

Our next point of grammar involves the present tense forms of the verb *to be*. In English these forms are *am, art, is* and *are*. Hebrew *has* such forms, but almost never *uses* them, except in reference to God, or when absolutely necessary for context. The reason for this may be that the forms are too close to God's name in Hebrew. While this may seem awkward to us, there are many other languages that don't use the present tense of the verb to be. Russian, for example, has become so used to ignoring the forms, that some of them are completely obsolete. The Russian equivalent of *am* can't even be found in a dictionary or grammar book anymore. They get along fine without it, and so does Hebrew. But English can't, so we have to insert the appropriate forms when translating. *And a man who will lie down with a male in a woman's bed, both of them have done an abomination; dying they will be put to death, their blood is.*

בם *bam* - This word is a contraction. Unlike English contractions, no apostrophe is needed. It is formed by taking the preposition ב *b*, which means *in*, and which cannot exist as a separate word, and attaching it to the final letter of the pronominal ending הם *hem*. The resulting word means *in them*. As mentioned earlier, Hebrew doesn't always use prepositions the way we do, and this is one case where English would use a different preposition to express the same concept. We would use *on*, so we will translate the word as *on them*. *And a man who will lie down with a male in a woman's bed, both of them have done an abomination; dying they will be put to death, their blood is on them.*

This is the correct translation of Leviticus 20:13. It can be seen that, rather than forbidding male homosexuality, it simply forbids two males to lie down in a woman's bed, for whatever reason. Culturally, a woman's bed was her own. Other than the woman herself, only her husband was permitted in her bed, and there were even restrictions on when he was allowed in there. Any other use of her bed would have been considered defilement. Other verses in the Law will help clarify the acceptable use of the woman's bed. (Lev. 15).

Romans 1:26-27

Διὰ τοῦτο παρέδωκεν αὐτοὺς ὁ Θεὸς εἰς πάθη ἀτιμίας· αἵ τε γὰρ θήλειαι αὐτῶν μετήλλαξαν τὴν φυσικὴν χρῆσιν εἰς τὴν παρὰ φύσιν, ὁμοίως τε καὶ οἱ ἄρσενες ἀφέντες τὴν φυσικὴν χρῆσιν τῆς θηλείας ἐξεκαύθησαν ἐν τῇ ὀρέξει αὐτῶν εἰς ἀλλήλους ἄρσενες ἐν ἄρσενιν, τὴν ἀσχημοσύνην κατεργαζόμενοι καὶ τὴν ἀντιμισθίαν ἣν ἔδει τῆς πλάνης αὐτῶν ἐν αὐτοῖς ἀπολαμβάνοντες.

Dhia touto paredhoken aftous o Theos eis pathi atimias ai te gar thiliai afton metillaxan tin fisikin chrisin is tin para fisin, omios te kai i arsenes afentes tin fisikin chrisin tis thilias exekavthisan en ti orexi afton is allilus arsenes en arsesin, tin aschimosinin katergazomeni kai tin antimisthian in edhi tis planis afton en aftis apolamvanontes.

(Modern Greek transliteration)

"Through this, God gave them over to passions of dishonor: their women exchanged the natural use into one against nature. Likewise, also the males left the natural use of the female, burned in their lust for each other, males in males, committing an unseemliness, receiving in themselves the appropriate reward for their error."

One of the biggest mistakes Christians make with Paul's epistle to the church at Rome is their failure to comprehend Romans 1:7... Paul's epistle was addressed to a specific group of people in the first century, *not* to everyone in the twenty-first century. Are we saying that the epistle doesn't apply to us at all? Of course not: it certainly applies to every age and nation. But what verse 7 reminds us is that when we read the epistle, we need to keep in mind that it was written to first century Rome, and applies first and foremost to the situations that were extant then.

So what *was* going on in Rome? The ancient Greek and Roman concept of what was normal and moral was quite different from ours. Although such concepts as *sexual orientation* had not been studied or named, in behavior, both the Greek and Roman cultures expected everyone to be bisexual. There were very specific rules regarding how this worked: A woman, for example, was expected to have one husband, and was not permitted sexual contact with any other man. But sexual contact with other women was permitted and even *expected*. For a man, the rules permitted him wives, and perhaps even concubines, depending on his wealth. But an adult man would also be "attached" to an adolescent male, to whom he would be teacher, mentor and lover.

An example of this type of relationship can be seen in Matthew chapter 8. The King James Version incorrectly has the centurion referring to his "servant." But he never called him his servant. (The person in question was a servant, or perhaps a slave, but that information is from a third person reference to him, not what the centurion said about him.) The centurion called him *"my boy."* This would not have been his son, because a man wouldn't refer to his son with the word παις (pronounced a bit like the English word *pace*), even though that was the usual word for a boy. To refer to one's own son that way would have been seen as disrespectful. Rather, παις was the common word used by a Greek or Roman to refer to his adolescent partner. Jesus, having grown up under Roman occupation, would have understood the nature of this relationship. He said not a word about it, but admired the centurion's faith and healed the boy.

Any man or women in Roman society who had relations with only one gender would have been thought odd or even abnormal. The origin of this phenomenon was actually the creation myth shared by the Greeks and Romans. This taught that there was originally only one human, who was not male or female as we understand the terms. This human was split into two by divine intervention. One of the two was now male, the other female. (This really isn't too different from the account found in the Hebrew text of Genesis.) But to their mind, this meant that each individual was now inherently "incomplete." The male lacked his female half, the female lacked her male half. They sought a means to restore wholeness.[20] Although on the surface it would seem that they would conclude that being united sexually with someone of the opposite sex would accomplish that, in actual practice, they determined that the best way to do it was for each person to be intimate with *both* sexes. This began, centuries earlier, as a religious obligation, and had grown into a custom/expectation. But under the Romans, it had evidently evolved into a convenient outlet for unbridled lust. Whereas in earlier times, those participating in the custom would have undoubtedly felt uncomfortable engaging in sexual relations with someone to whom they had no natural attraction, under the Romans, sexual orientation became irrelevant, and they just lusted indiscriminately. Paul basically said that God had

---

[20] Aristophanes's Speech from Plato's *Symposium*

just given them over to it, enabling them to completely disregard their natural attractions.

The biggest difficulty with such a societal expectation, of course, is that, by nature, most people are *not* bisexual. This means that almost everyone had to violate their own sexual orientation in order to fit in. In the above verses, we can see that Paul spoke of the Roman women "exchanging" the natural use for one that was "παρα φυσιν" *against nature*. Now please understand what Paul meant by *nature*: He was not speaking of nature as creation. (Indeed, homosexuality, as well as bisexuality, exists throughout nature, in many hundreds of animal species.)[21] Rather, the Greek noun φυσις refers to *a person's* (or *thing's*) **own** nature or natural disposition. What Paul was addressing was the Romans' ***own*** nature in regard to sexual behavior, what we today would call their sexual orientation. Their society was expecting everyone to trade ("exchange") their own orientation, whatever it might have been, for a bisexual orientation. And what they were doing was dishonorable and unseemly (out of character), and a mistake, not because of the concept of homosexuality, but because they were violating the way they were created.

Romans chapter one, as a whole, deals with pagan Rome's

---

[21] Bagemihl, Ph.D., Bruce. "Biological Exuberance: Animal Homosexuality and Natural Diversity." New York. St. Martin's Press. 2000.

attempts to turn the creation into a god, worshiping the things created rather than the One who created them. They were attempting to remake that creation in their own design by ignoring the inborn sexual orientation of the people and expecting them to live bisexually. This chapter is not about homosexuality vs. heterosexuality, but rather about the error of trying to change the way we were created. God has given each of us a sexual orientation, and for us to attempt to change it into another one is, in effect, telling God that He created us wrong. But if it was wrong for heterosexuals and homosexuals in the first century to try to be bisexuals, then it is equally wrong, and for the same reasons, for homosexuals in the twenty-first century to try to be heterosexuals, or vice-versa.

There may be some who would doubt that heterosexuals in the first century would live a bisexual lifestyle simply to satisfy the misguided expectations of society. To such people we say this: *Look around you... all over the world, there are homosexual people trying to live a heterosexual lifestyle for exactly the same reason.* And the societies and the religions trying to force them to do so are just as misguided. The same God who created homosexuality, heterosexuality, and bisexuality throughout the animal kingdom, did the same thing with us.

1 Corinthians 6:9 & 1 Timothy 1:10

These verses are mistranslated in pretty much every English Bible commonly available. Both verses are printed below in Greek, then transliterated, and correctly translated, with explanations about the translations.

1 Corinthians 6:9

Ἢ οὐκ οἴδατε ὅτι ἄδικοι Θεοῦ βασιλείαν οὐ κληρονομήσουσιν; Μὴ πλανᾶσθε· οὔτε πόρνοι οὔτε εἰδωλολάτραι οὔτε μοιχοὶ οὔτε μαλακοὶ οὔτε ἀρσενοκοῖται...

I ouk idhate oti adhiki Theou vasilian ou klironomisousin? Mi planasthe; oute porni oute idhololatrai oute mikhi oute malaki oute arsenokitai...

(Transliteration of Modern Greek pronunciation.)

Or haven't you known that the unjust will not inherit the kingdom of God? Do not be misled; neither fornicators nor idolaters nor adulterers nor soft ones* nor those who lie with males...**

1 Timothy 1:10

πόρωοις, ἀρσενοκοίταις, ἀνδραποδισταῖς, ψεύσταις, ἐπιόρκοις, καὶ εἴ τι ἕτερον τῇ ὑγιαινούσῃ διδασκαλίᾳ ἀντίκειται,

...*pornis, arsenokitais, andhrapodhistais, psevstais, epiorkis, kei i ti eterov ti iyi-einousi dhidhaskalia antikitai,*

(Transliteration of Modern Greek pronunciation.)

...to fornicators, to those who lie with males,** to kidnappers, to liars, to perjurers, and if any other thing opposes healthful teaching,

*Soft ones: The Greek word μαλακοὶ (*mala-KEE)* is a plural noun, derived from the adjective μαλακός (*mala-KOS).* The adjective means infirm (from illness), or soft or fine, but in meaning soft or fine, is restricted to describing material or clothing. It describes the type of clothing worn by very wealthy people. This adjective was used in Luke 7:25, when

Jesus asked the crowd if they had gone out to the wilderness expecting to see someone dressed in fine clothing. A noun derived from this adjective was most often used to mean people who are ill. Alternately, it would seem to suggest the type of people who wore soft or fine clothing, which, in the first century, would be the very rich. Jesus Himself indicated how difficult it would be for wealthy people to enter the kingdom. (Luke 18:24)

Those who lie with males: The Greek word ἀρσενοκοῖται (*arseno-KEE-tay*) (the form used in 1 Timothy is ἀρσενοκοίταις [*arseno-KEE-tays*]), is formed by combining a form of the noun αρσην *arsin*, which means *male*, with the construction κοιτ *kit-*, a derivative of the verb κειμαι *kimei*, which means *lie down*. Combined, the word refers to *people who lie down with males*. What remains to be determined is whether the word is referring to *males* lying with males, or *females* lying with males. Ordinarily, to determine if a Greek noun is masculine or feminine, one looks at it in the nominative case with the definite article. For example, ὁ ἀδελφός - *o adhelfos*, *the brother*, is in the nominative case, and both the *os* ending and the definite article ὁ tell us the noun is masculine. But the word used in these two verses presents a small challenge to us, because in first century

69

literature, it never appears with a definite article. (In fact, outside these two passages, it never appears at all!) Of course, we could simply look it up in a modern Greek dictionary, and it would tell us the word is masculine and means *homosexual*. But is that the end of it? Actually, no. The dictionary's definition and assignment of gender are based on centuries of preconceived notions about what Paul was saying, and not on actual usage from the first century. So in this case, the dictionary can't answer the question for us. We need to look back to the word itself, and its context, to search for clues.

The last two letters of the word in 1 Corinthians, and the last three in 1 Timothy, are where we need to look first. Greek nouns are declined according to case. That is, the ending of a noun changes to indicate how the word is being used in the sentence. We have something similar with English pronouns: We use the word *I* as a subject, but *me* as an object. For all intents and purposes, *I* and *me* mean the same thing. But it is incorrect to say *Me want a book*, or *Give I a book*. In 1 Corinthians, the word is in the nominative case, and the ending is one that is often feminine. This would suggest that the word is referring to *women* lying with males. In 1 Timothy, the word is in the dative case, which in English corresponds to putting the word *to* before the noun. (Example: Give the book *TO ME*.) And again, the ending is one that is often feminine.

The fact that this word is not found in any literature prior to the first century, and then only in Paul's two uses, suggests that Paul himself coined it. Although there was no such word as *homosexual* at the time, there were expressions in common use to indicate sexual activity between persons of the same sex. Had Paul intended to refer to homosexuals here, common sense would have him use expressions people already knew and understood. But he never used any of those expressions in his writing. So the creation of a new word suggests a different concept. In addition, had he intended for his new word to be understood to refer to males, he would have given it a different ending: The plural ending οι (οις in the dative case) is never feminine, and would have served just that purpose. But he didn't do that, either. So even without a definite article to prove the point, the evidence so far suggests that Paul was speaking about *women* when he used this word, not men.

There is more evidence to consider: First, when properly translated, scripture contains no prior condemnation of homosexuality, and the Hebrew Old Testament contains the record of two same-sex marriages, neither condemned by God. Paul, as a Jewish scholar, could not have been ignorant of this. So for him to suddenly, and without precedent, introduce a condemnation of homosexuality, without a word of explanation, would make absolutely no sense, and would probably have created an uproar in the early churches. Church history documents that same-sex marriages existed, and continued, in the Christian churches up until around the 13th or 14th century.[22]

This word was used only twice in the first century, both times by Paul, and was not used again until the second century. In the second century, writers used it to mean female prostitutes.[23] This raises the question of why Paul would create a new word for prostitutes. A valid reason for doing so was that he had already used the original word for prostitutes to mean something else. Centuries before, in earliest Greek, the πορν– *(porn-)* root referred only to prostitutes and prostitution. But over the centuries, it had expanded in meaning, and now referred to any extra-marital sex. Paul had already used the word πόρνοι to mean *fornicators*. Since prostitution was both a business and a form of worship of the fertility goddess, some could have argued that Paul didn't have prostitutes in mind when he said fornicators. So the word ἀρσενοκοῖται covers that loophole. In later centuries, at least one writer understood the word to mean something a

---

[22] "Same-Sex Unions in Premodern Europe" by John Boswell.
[23] Sibylline Oracles 2.70-77, Acts of John, Theophilus of Antioch's Ad Autolycum

husband did with his wife.[24] Historically, only relatively recently have people begun to think this word referred to homosexuals, and newer translations actually render the word that way, despite the lack of grammatical or historical support.

Is it true that Paul coined ἀρσενοκοῖται from Lev. 20:13 in the Septuagint?

There is a misconception currently held by some Christians that Paul coined the word ἀρσενοκοῖται from Lev. 20:13 as found in the Greek Septuagint (LXX), which is the oldest translation of the Hebrew Bible.:

Και ος αν κοιμηθη μετα αρσενος κοιτην γυναικος βδελυγμα εποιησαν αμφοτεροι θανατουσθωσαν ενοχοι εισιν·

The idea is based upon the existence of the words **αρσενος κοιτην** in that verse, but this is flawed scholarship. Since αρσενος means *male*, and κοιτην means *bed*, ANY Greek sentence that mentions *a male* and *a bed* will have forms of those two words in it. Leviticus 18:22 and 20:13 are not the only verses in the Septuagint containing those words, as seen below.

Και νυν αποκτεινατε παν αρσενικον εν παση τη απαρτια

---

[24] John the Faster, Patriarch of Constantinople, "Penitential." circa AD 575.

και πασαν γυναικα ητις εγνωκεν **κοιτην αρσενος** ζωγρησατε αυτας

Πασαν την απαρτιαν των γυναικων ητις ουκ οιδεν **κοιτην αρσενος** ζωγρησατε αυτας

*And now kill every male among all children. But every woman who has not known **the bed of a male**, take them alive. All the women children who have not gone to **the bed of a male**, take them alive.*

Num. 31:17-18

Και ουτος ο λογος ον ποιησετε παν αρσενικον και πασαν γυναικα γινωσκουσαν **κοιτην αρσενος** αναθεματιετε

Και ευρον απο των κατοικουντων ιαβις γαλααδ τετρακοσιας νεανιδας παρθενους αι ουκ εγνωσαν ανδρα εις **κοιτην αρσενος** και ηγον αυτας εις την παρεμβολης εις σηλω η εστιν εν γη χανααν

*And this is the word that you will do: every male, and every woman who has known **the bed of a male**, you will destroy. And they found among the inhabitants of Jabesh Gilead four hundred young virgins who had not known a man in **the bed of a male**, and the brought them into the camp into Shiloh which is in the land of Canaan.*

Judges 21:11-12

In each of these four verses, the phrase "bed of a male" is in relation to women who have not known that location, that is, women who were virgins.

In Leviticus, however, we have a different set up. Lev. 20:13 includes the phrase **μετα αρσενος κοιτην γυναικος**. In this verse, αρσενος (a male) is preceded by μετα (with), while κοιτην (a bed) is paired with the genitive γυναικος (of a woman). This agrees exactly with the Hebrew text, that is, **with a male** (in) **a woman's bed**.

Ἀρσενοκοῖται, on the other hand, is NOT derived from the word for *bed*, but from the verb meaning *"lie down."* This verb, κειμαι, in some of its forms, uses the construction κοιτ-. Therefore, ἀρσενοκοῖται does not mean *male beds,* but rather, *those who lie with males.*

Same-Sex Marriage in Scripture

In this chapter, we will examine biblical precedent for same-sex marriage. Prior to searching, it would be prudent to lay some groundwork, starting with the definition of the word "marriage." The modern concept of marriage is this: a couple with a government-issued license, making vows before a minister, priest, rabbi, other clergyman, or a justice of the peace. Such a concept of marriage is relatively modern, and does not match the biblical concept of marriage.

Perhaps the most important difference between biblical marriage and its modern day counterpart is that, in biblical times, government did not regulate marriage. There was no such thing as a marriage license, nor did the government care who married whom, or how many spouses a person had.

The early concept of marriage was this: two people made a covenant[25] with each other. Regardless of whether they did

---

[25] בְּרִית - b'rit

this of their own accord, or through a matchmaker, or at the insistence of their families, the marriage began with the agreement or covenant between the two. Some time afterward, there would be a feast for public recognition of the agreement, and a contract[26] would be signed by both parties, putting in writing what they had already promised to each other. After this was done, and only then, would the couple live together and be intimate with each other. Prior to the signing of the contract, the couple was spoken of as betrothed or engaged, but this had a meaning different from today's concept of betrothal or engagement. Their betrothal was as morally binding as the marriage itself, and could only be broken by divorce, even though no contract had been signed and no sexual activity had occurred.

An example of this can be seen in Matthew 1:19, with Joseph and Mary. At this point in their relationship, they were only betrothed. They had not moved in together, had not signed a contract, had not had a marriage feast, and had not had sexual contact. All they had was the agreement they had made with each other, their covenant. But when Joseph discovered that Mary was pregnant, he thought she had been unfaithful, and decided not to marry her, but instead to

---

[26] כְּתוּבָּה – ketubah, "something written." Broyde, Michael and Jonathan Reiss. "The Value and Significance of the Ketubah." Journal of Halacha and Contemporary Society, XLVII. 2004.

divorce her privately. (The King James Version says *"put her away."* The Greek word is ἀπολῦσαι *apolysai*, and it means *divorce*.) Even though they had none of the things that would make a modern marriage binding, they were considered married, simply on the basis of their agreement with each other! So for a biblical definition of marriage we have simply one thing: a covenant. When two people make an agreement between themselves that they will live their lives together as a couple and be faithful to each other, then, biblically, they are married. They may choose to sign a contract, they may choose to have a ceremony and reception, they may choose any other forms of public recognition, but none of those are required biblically for the marriage to be binding.

One final point before we search scripture for examples of same-sex marriage: We'll be using primarily the King James Version of scripture, with corrections to translation errors provided by the Hebrew and Greek texts. It needs to be understood by the reader that words that appear in *italics* in the King James Version are not found in the Hebrew or Greek text, but were added by the translators. Sometimes those added words help clarify a concept, and adding an occasional article *(a, an, the)* or preposition is a valid part of translation. Literal word-for-word translation is usually impossible and rarely desirable. For example, let us take the Hebrew word

ובמשכנותיך *uv'mish'k'noteicha*. Even though it is only one word in Hebrew, it is impossible to translate it into English with less than four words. It means *and in thy tabernacles*.

But sometimes the added words of the translators do us a disservice. Sometimes they completely change the meaning (which is often what they intended to do.) For example, look at Colossians 1:19 in the King James Version. Notice that the words *the Father* are in italics. Other translations may have the word *God* where the King James has *the Father*. But the Greek text mentions neither. The verse in Greek says *For all the fullness was pleased to dwell in Him*. By inserting *the Father* or *God*, the translators changed the meaning of what Paul wrote. Not only is that not helpful, it's sinful! (Rev. 22:18-19)

In I Samuel chapter 18, Jonathan met David and loved him immediately. Verse 1 tells us that the soul of Jonathan was knit, or intertwined, with the soul of David. Lest we think of this simply as something spiritual, let us look at the meaning of *soul*. There is an erroneous conception that the soul is similar to, or synonymous with, the spirit. Some preachers try to turn us into a sort of trinity, claiming that we are made up of three parts, that is, body, soul and spirit. But the scripture does not say this. We know from Genesis 2:7 that God formed our bodies out of the dust of the earth. It then says in the same verse that He breathed into our nostrils the breath of life, i.e., spirit, and man BECAME a living soul. (In Hebrew, Greek and some other languages, the words for *wind* and *spirit* are the same.) So the formula isn't

BODY + SOUL + SPIRIT = MAN,

but rather,

BODY + SPIRIT = SOUL.

Therefore, when the soul of Jonathan was knit with the soul of David, it was not simply a spiritual thing; it was physical as well. Jonathan loved David with body and spirit.

I Samuel 18:3-4 tell us that Jonathan and David made a covenant, and that, to seal the covenant, Jonathan took off all the things he was wearing and gave them to David. The things he took off tell us a lot about the covenant itself. He took off his sword and bow and gave them to David, perhaps suggesting that he intended to protect David. But it went further than that. By taking off all his clothes, he signified a much deeper and more intense relationship. Had this not been the start of a physical, sexual relationship, Jonathan's actions would have been considered bizarre indeed, by the standards of their day, or ours. (The Hebrew does list everything Jonathan would have been wearing, with the possible exception of a loincloth. A loincloth, however, was unlikely given the circumstances: They had just come from the battlefield. In battle, a soldier needed to be able to relieve himself quickly. This is part of the reason the army uniform worn was much shorter than the full-length robes worn in everyday life. A loincloth would have caused unnecessary hindrance to the process of urinating quickly in urgent circumstances.)

From that day, David moved in with Saul and Jonathan (verse 2) and did not live at home with his parents anymore, further indicative of the type of covenant they had made. (In biblical times, a man generally did not leave his parents' home until he married, and sometimes not even then.) Although it was Saul who insisted that David move in, this is not something he would have done on his own. Living in the king's house was reserved for family and a few servants. Although David was a national hero, Saul was not the type of man willing to share the fame. On the contrary, he was prone to jealousy. The last thing he would have wanted to do was call extra attention to David by having him live in the king's house. But when Jonathan and David made a covenant, Saul was more or less obligated to invite David to move in.

At this point, we need to clarify something before going on: It needs to be understood that today's concept of monogamy was not considered the norm in biblical days. Especially among royalty, polygamy was considered essential in order to produce many heirs, which would ensure that the throne would remain in the same family. Jonathan was the eldest son of the king, and had a responsibility to produce *at least* one heir to the throne. He did so. The prophet Samuel had anointed David to be king. This placed the obligation of producing an heir upon him as well. King Saul was well aware that Samuel had anointed David, and he warned his son that as long as David lived, he (Jonathan) would never be king. This is why the relationship between the two young men bothered Saul so much. The very reason he had fathered Jonathan was so that his son would succeed him as king, and now Jonathan was thwarting that purpose by becoming involved with the only man who threatened that royal succession!

Saul sought a way to get rid of David. Because David was anointed, and was also very popular, it would have been inadvisable for Saul to attempt to kill him outright (not that he didn't try). Rather, he preferred that the Philistines do it for him. He reasoned within himself that if he got David to marry his daughter Merab, she would cause him enough distraction that he would fall to his enemies.[27] But when the time came

---

[27] 1 Samuel 18:17

for David and Merab to make a covenant, she married someone else instead.[28] (Although he expressed his lack of worthiness to marry Merab, David raised no actual objection to the marriage, so most likely Merab herself objected. Perhaps she did so because she cared about David and understood her father's ulterior motive, or perhaps she was in love with the man she married.) Then Saul learned that another of his daughters, Michal, loved David. He decided to let her marry David, again for the sole purpose of causing him to fall to his enemies.[29]

When Saul told David that he would give him Michal, he went on to tell David that once he married her, he would be the king's son-in-law **"in *one of* the twain."** (1 Sam. 18:21b - King James Version) That phrase is very important. Let's put it into modern English first: **"through *one of* the two."** This seems to suggest that David would be Saul's son-in-law through Michal instead of Merab. But notice that the words '*one of*' are in italics. That means they are not found in the Hebrew text. In fact, they are not even *hinted at* in the Hebrew text. Adding them completely changed the meaning of the verse. What Saul actually told David was this:

ויאמר שאול אל דוד בשתיים תתחתן בי היום:

Va'yomer Sha'ul el David bishta'yim titchaten bi ha'yom

---

[28] 1 Samuel 18:19

[29] 1 Samuel 18:20-21

And Saul said to David, "Today you will be my son-in-law through two."[30]

That is, he would be the king's son-in-law twice, through two of Saul's children. With which of Saul's children did David have a covenant? Only three of Saul's children are mentioned: Jonathan, Merab and Michal. David made no covenant with Merab, who married someone else. He was about to make a covenant with Michal. The only other child of Saul with whom David had a covenant was Jonathan. Verse 21 proves that the covenant was a marriage covenant and that Saul recognized (but clearly didn't approve of) the marriage.

Note the following verses that the King James and other English Bibles have mistranslated in relation to the marriage of David and Jonathan:

I Samuel 20:30 –

ויחר־אף שאול ביהונתן ויאמר לו בן־נעות המרדות הלוא ידעתי כי־בחר אתה לבן־ישי לבשתך ולבשת ערות אמך

Vayichar af Sha'ul bihonatan vayomer lo ben na'avat hamardut halo yadati ki vocher atah l'ven Yishai l'vosht'cha ul'voshet ervat imecha

"Then Saul's anger burned toward Jonathan, and he said

---

[30] At least one English version, rather than adding words to change the meaning, mistranslated the word "two" as "the second," again to imply that Saul meant through Michal instead of Merab. That translation is also incorrect, as the word for "two" does not mean "second" in Hebrew.

to him, you son of the perversion of rebelliousness! Don't I know that you are choosing the son of Jesse to your own shame and the shame of your mother's _____*?"

*_____ There is no polite English word for the one King Saul used. He used a graphic and vulgar term for genitalia.

I Samuel 20:41 –

הנער בא ודוד קם מאצל הנגב ויפל לאפיו ארצה וישתחו שלש פעמים וישקו איש את־רעהו ויבכו איש את־רעהו עד־דוד הגדיל

Hana'ar ba v'David kam me'etzel hanegev vayipol l'apav artzah vayishtachu shalosh p'amim vayishku ish et re'ehu vayivku ish et re'ehu ad David higdil.

"The boy went, and David came up from the south, and fell on his face to the ground, and they bowed three times, and kissed each other, and wept with each other, until David experienced an erection*."

*Hebrew: הגדיל *Higdil: became large, was made large; euphemistically, an erection*

In II Samuel, 1:26, David expressed his love for the late Jonathan. It is important to understand that when David referred to the *love of women*, the only possible love he could have been referring to was sexual love. It was considered highly improper for a man to have a platonic friendship with a woman. Men and women usually didn't even speak to each other in public. Even a husband and wife would not speak to each other in the street. (Some Chassidic Jews still observe this custom.) Since David would not have had any platonic relationships with women, he could only have been referring to sexual interaction. This is a further indication of the sexual nature of his relationship with Jonathan, since it would not make sense to compare a platonic relationship with a man to a sexual relationship with a woman. David clearly preferred the love of Jonathan. Nowhere in scripture will you find David expressing such love for a woman. Although he lusted after women (suggesting he was bisexual), married more than once, and fathered children, he never expressed such love for any of his wives.

Having found one example of same-sex marriage, let's look at another:

In Daniel 1:3, we meet Ashpenaz, chief of the Babylonian eunuchs. He was put in charge of the new eunuchs brought in from Judah, the princes and chief young men who had been castrated in fulfillment of prophecy (II Kings 20:18; Isaiah 39:7). Among these were Daniel, Shadrach, Meshach and

Abednego. All four were eunuchs.

Before going on, we need to discuss the concept of eunuchs and the effect of castration. Were eunuchs capable of sexual function? There is no set answer to the question. It depends upon when they were castrated. Boys castrated before puberty, as was sometimes done to keep their singing voices from changing, would not develop sexually and would have no sexual function. They would still have normal desire for physical and emotional closeness, but could not function sexually. Those castrated after puberty would be sterile, but would most likely retain some sexual function and desire. This can be seen in the case of cats. A male kitten castrated before puberty does not develop sexually, and usually will not display any of the behaviors of adult male cats, such as spraying to mark territory, and mounting other cats. Male cats castrated after puberty will often continue to spray and to mount other cats, but will be sterile.

(Note that in Bible times, male eunuchs were not permitted to marry women, since heterosexual marriage carried with it an expectation of procreation, but as we shall see, were permitted relationships with men.)

What about Daniel, Shadrach, Meshach and Abednego? The prophecy spoke of the *young men* of Judah, not boys. The fact that Daniel and the others were able to speak for themselves and stand up for themselves indicates they were at least in their teens. So it seems fairly evident that these young men were castrated after, or at least during, puberty, and would therefore retain some sexual function. We have no information from scripture about the personal lives of Shadrach, Meshach and Abednego. But scripture does give us some clues as to Daniel's personal life.

Daniel 1:9 –

ויתן האלהים את־דניאל לחסד ולרחמים לפני שר הסריסים

Vayiten ha'Elohim et Daniyel l'chesed ul'rachamim lifnei sar hasarisim

"Now God had brought Daniel into favor and tender love with the prince of the eunuchs." (KJV)

In this verse, we find that a certain relationship existed between Daniel and Ashpenaz, chief of the eunuchs. (His name was mentioned in verse 3.) To determine the exact nature of that relationship, we'll need to dig a little deeper than the English translations, which actually tell us only a little. The King James speaks of *favor* and *tender love*. The Hebrew words are חסד *chesed* and רחמים *rachamim*. Let's look at *chesed* first. This word has more than one possible translation. The most common is *mercy*. It may also be translated as *grace* or *favor*. The scriptures that say '*His mercy endureth forever*' use a form of the word *chesed*.[31]

What about *rachamim*? This word also has more than one meaning. Additionally, it is plural, which has more than one connotation in Hebrew. Let's deal with that aspect first, before determining the meaning. In Hebrew, using the plural can be a way of emphasizing greatness or importance. Indeed, there are some Hebrew nouns that have no singular form, but are always plural: *Heaven, water, life,* and *face* are words that have no singular form in Hebrew, but are always plural.[32] In addition, God, when referring to the true God, is usually plural in Hebrew, not because He is more than one, but in order to emphasize His greatness. *Rachamim* is plural, not because it is more than one, but because of its greatness, intensity or depth.

So what does it mean? There are two common meanings for the word *rachamim*. One is similar to the meaning of *chesed*, that is, *mercy* or *grace*. The other is *love*. (More on that in a moment.) How would a reader determine which meaning is intended? From context: Since the word *chesed* was also used, for *rachamim* to have the meaning of *mercy* would be redundant. It being plural would be even more

---

[31] לְעוֹלָם חַסְדּוֹ - l'olam chasdo

[32] שמים מים חיים פנים – shamayim, mayim, chayim, panim – heaven, water, life, face

redundant. Therefore, *rachamim* would default to its alternate meaning, *love*. But what kind of love? English is poor in that we only have one word for love, and must use other words to differentiate between types of love. The love between spouses is not the same as love between parents and children. The love between parents and children is not the same as love between friends. And yet, we have just the one word, *love*. Some languages, including Hebrew and Greek, have more than one word for love. For example, the passage in John 21 where Jesus kept asking Peter *"Do you love me?"* is much more significant if read in Greek: Peter was answering Jesus with the wrong word for love, embarrassed by the fact that Jesus was using a far more powerful word for love. Peter was basically answering, *"Yes, I like you!"*

Words in Hebrew are formed from root words, usually made up of three letters. Any words having those three letters, in that same order, would have related meanings. For example, most people are familiar with the word שלום *shalom*, which means *peace* or *well-being*. The root letters are ש-ל-ם *SH - L - M*. Any word with ש-ל-ם, in that order, regardless of other consonants or vowels added, would have a related meaning. The root letters of *rachamim* are ר-ח-ם *R-CH-M* (the final *im* of *rachamim* make it plural, and are not part of the root). There are a number of Hebrew words that share these root letters, including two organs of reproduction. This fact indicates that when *rachamim* is used to mean *love*, it has a definite physical, sexual aspect to it.

At this point, we would like the reader to notice who was responsible for Daniel and Ashpenaz having a sexual relationship: According to verse 9, it was **God** who put them together in their relationship. Now God has no vested interest in people committing fornication, and the fact that *rachamim* means sexual *love*, and not just sexual *activity*, indicates to us that this was meant to be a life-long relationship between the two. And what do we call a life-long committed sexual relationship between two people? Marriage. No other romantic interest or sexual partner or marriage was ever mentioned in connection with Daniel in the Bible; Ashpenaz was the only one.

We have two examples of same-sex marriage from scripture. But what rules should govern these marriages? It is true that scripture does not give us rules specifically governing same-sex marriages. Does that mean we are free to make our own? Not necessarily. Notice again in 1 Samuel 18 that King Saul didn't seem to draw any distinction between David's marriage to Jonathan and his impending marriage to Michal. Although Saul didn't approve of the first marriage, he still recognized it as a marriage. Therefore, it seems evident that the instructions given in the Bible for opposite-sex marriages were also meant to be applied to same-sex marriages.

Transgender

Contrary to what some people think, this is a medical issue, NOT a moral issue. Sadly, some try to oversimplify things with statements like *"God makes everyone male or female,"* or *"If the chromosomes are XY, it's a male, if they are XX, it's a female."* Some will quote Genesis 1:27 and 5:2, "...He created them male and female...," overlooking the fact that the "them" referred to in those verses was Adam and Eve, NOT the entire human race. God only created two humans from "scratch." The rest of us were born according to the rules of biology and genetics.

These above simplistic statements overlook the plain fact that children are frequently born with no clear physical sex, either having the organs of both, or organs that don't clearly indicate either sex. They also ignore the fact that the human race is not neatly divided into two groups, one with XY

chromosomes, and one with XX. There are a number of sex chromosome disorders:
- 47,XXX
- 48, XXXX
- 49 XXXXY syndrome
- 49, XXXXX
- Klinefelter's syndrome, XXY
- Turner syndrome, X
- XX gonadal dysgenesis
- XX male syndrome
- XXYY syndrome
- XYY syndrome

So clearly, the human race is not neatly divided into two groups as some believe.

Sex differentiation begins in the first trimester of pregnancy. Besides disorders of chromosomes, other things can influence this negatively. For example, if the pregnant woman is exposed to extraneous hormones, this can negatively affect the developing embryo, whether the source of the hormones is external, or something created by her own body.

Another unusual event that could occur early in pregnancy, probably before implantation of the blastocyst that will become the embryo, is the joining of two blastocysts into one. If there are two fertilized ova, one genetically male, the other female, and they attach to each other, they can merge to the point of becoming one embryo... but that embryo may have the chromosomes of both sexes, and even the organs of both sexes.

Gender identity is separate from physical sex, although probably develops at the same time, and is undoubtedly initiated by the same sequence of events. But just as things can go wrong with the development of physical sex, so too things can go wrong with the development of gender identity, and it is possible for an individual to be born with a gender identity that does not match the physical sex, even if there is no detectable underlying chromosomal abnormality.

A couple of points before going on: Gender identity and sexual orientation are entirely unrelated things. When determined from the standpoint of gender identity, the great majority of transgender individuals are heterosexual. Second, despite the misconceptions of some, gender identity is not the product of environment. If it were, we would be unlikely to see any transgender people at all. But when one is confronted with a child of three or four, who has been raised according to physical sex, who insists, despite all evidence to the contrary, that he or she is the other sex, it becomes apparent that there is more to it than upbringing. Now, this is not the same as, for example, a stage some girls may go through where they wish they were boys. Wishing to be the opposite sex, for whatever reason or for however long, is a far cry from believing that one actually is the opposite sex.

A person who is transgender tends to have that sense of "wrongness," usually from earliest memory, and will have a firm, unshakeable knowledge of being the gender opposite of that suggested by physical organs. Such a person cannot be "talked out" of the conviction, nor is it something to be masked with psychotropic medication. Medical science has no means at present to alter a person's gender identity. It appears to be fixed prior to birth and immutable. So the only solution it can offer is SRS - Sex Reassignment Surgery, although not all transgender persons opt for it. (For many, the cost is prohibitive, and it's rarely covered by insurance.)

It bears mentioning, since there are unlearned people who often claim otherwise, that people who have undergone SRS are generally quite happy with their decision, and are much less likely to be depressed than those who have not. It also bears mentioning that transitioning while young has significant advantages, particularly for those transitioning from male to female. During puberty, male hormones are responsible for the growth of facial hair, broad shoulders, voice change, subtle developments of the brow and perhaps jawline, size of hands, and even height. And these changes are not desirable for a person who identifies as female! So parents of a transgender child who allow their child to dress according to gender identity, and to take a puberty-blocking medication[33], are not negligent or abusive, but doing their child a tremendous favor. It's also important to understand that a person cannot self-diagnose as transgender and walk into a doctor's office and get hormones and arrange for SRS. A professional diagnosis is required.

From time to time, a child is born with a cleft palate or club foot, or even a serious heart defect. With very few exceptions, nobody would object to surgery to correct such things. (There are some few whose religious beliefs would insist that parents rely solely on faith in such cases.) But the majority of people would never suggest that such surgeries, whether to save a life or to correct a deformity, were sin. So why is it that when the surgery involves genitalia some immediately assume there is sin involved?

Once it has been medically established that a person has a mismatch between physical sex and gender identity, transitioning (hormones, living as the target sex, and surgery) is no more sinful than surgery to correct a cleft palate. It

---

[33] Such drugs only delay puberty. They do not do anything that cannot later be reversed. Puberty can always be initiated at a later time if, for whatever reason, a person decides not to transition.

vastly improves the quality of life and hurts no one.

Scripture does not address this issue... just as it doesn't address many issues the writers didn't know about. But that doesn't mean it is wrong for us to address them, and deal with them according to the best medical knowledge available.

About the Author

William H. Carey is a retired Apostolic minister. He was cofounder of both the National Gay Pentecostal Alliance (NGPA) and the Apostolic Restoration Mission (ARM). He has worked in ministry in the LGBTQ community around the United States, and has published numerous books and tracts on topics including Church Administration, doctrine and the nature of the Godhead, published in English, and some also in Russian, Spanish, French and Hebrew.

Rev. Carey began studying Greek at the age of 11, and Hebrew at the age of 19. He taught beginning classes in both languages for many years. He attended Apostolic Pentecostal Bible School and Wide World of Truth Ministries Bible School (both formerly in Schenectady, NY), and wrote most of the ministerial training curriculum for the Apostolic Institute of ministry, the educational division of ARM.

A native of Brooklyn, NY, he attended high school in Galway, NY, and college in Schenectady and Albany, NY. He currently resides in Ferndale, Michigan with his husband, Larry.

Other books by this author include:

- **New Testament** – A new modern English translation of the Westcott-Hort Greek text
- **How Many is God?** – A short explanation of the difference between the Trinitarian doctrine and the teaching of Oneness
- **The Basics of New Testament Teaching: An Apostolic Guide to Doctrine**
- **Derailed** – The true story of how one man's ego and pride destroyed a mighty move of God
- **Repairing the Apostolic Church** – replacing the traditional Protestant model of church administration with the original Apostolic model.
- **Inside** – A novel (fantasy/fiction)

All titles available at http://stores.lulu.com/BroWCarey

Milton Keynes UK
Ingram Content Group UK Ltd.
UKHW041315060824
1175UKWH00058B/709